Looking in to Creich

Published by Bonar Bridge Local History Society©

ISBN 0-9553316-0-9

ISBN 978-0-9553316-0-2

The photograph on front cover - Dùn Creich - by Jacqueline M Fraser

Looking in to Creich

A survey of Gaelic Place Names in the Parish of Creich by Members of the Bonar Bridge Local History Society

Maps used. Ordnance Survey, Sheets 21 and 13, 1959 edition, 1:25,000 series.
Data as defined within parish boundaries.
Distance measured in miles. Height measured in feet.

Funding: Awards For All Scotland, and The Highland Council

Research and text provided by Marion Fraser.

Acknowledgements: The Society wishes to thank everyone who contributed, especially

Roddy Maclean Journalist, writer and broadcaster
Murdo Macleod, Honorary Librarian to The Gaelic Society of Inverness.
Ian M. Fraser, Chieftain of the Gaelic Society of Inverness.
Iain MacIllechiar of Gaelic Department UHI Inverness
The late **James Fraser** for information handed down through the oral tradition.
Mary Macdonald, for information on Norse derivations.
John Reid, computer advisor and format editor
Society members who took part in research and made photographs available.

About Bonar Bridge Local History Society

In the year 2000, a folk-memory exhibition of photographs in Bonar Bridge Village Hall organised by Bunty Gordon, provided me with a fine opportunity to gauge the level of interest in forming a history group. The research, in the shape of a questionnaire, gave a positive response and resulted in the formation of the Society at the inaugural meeting on 16th February 2001.

The object of the Society as laid out in the constitution is to stimulate interest and care for the history and the character of the area.

Secondly, to encourage the preservation of the development of features of historic importance, so in this regard we have improved access to facilitate viewing of St. Denham's Cross situated east of Creich cemetery.

Meetings and lectures are arranged and delegates attend conferences and training seminars.

It is intended that publications will be made available in keeping with the terms of the name of the Society.

A feature of the history society summer activity is the annual walk focusing on places of special interest as in 2001 the first such visit was to Càrn nam Fiatheach to look for the remains of a hill fort, believed to be one of many fortresses built to guard Tulloch district.

It is here that a hoard of early metalworks was found in 1900, although it is listed in The National Museum in Edinburgh, as the Migdale Hoard.

The skill of the early craftsmen in the district is exemplified in the find contained in the hoard, which included penannular bar armlets in bronze, along with tubular bronze beads, hair ornaments and other artefacts embellished with rows of vertical punch marks.

It was here in WW II that the Home Guard kept watch in readiness for a possible German invasion from the North.

The region North of Inverness was declared a protected area with barriers set up by the War Department, at Beauly for road users, and within the railway station in Inverness, where the required permit was examined.

The mid-summer walk in 2002 included a visit to Druim Liath the scene of a battle in 1013.

The year 2003 walkers visited various points of interest relating to the Gruinards massacre, which took place at the time of the Highland clearances.

During Highland Archaeology Week in October 2004 the society led a party of walkers to the summit of Dùn Creich, which was originally built to guard the waterway from invaders before there were roads.

The view from the 370ft. summit is regarded as one of the best in the Parish of Creich.

The 2005 June walk, in fine weather, did not attract so many walkers as those of previous years. The route starting from Carbisdale castle included a forest walk and a visit to the site of the Battle of Carbisdale on the Hill of Lamentation.

Now in 2006 it is business as usual, planning the June walk to Loch Laro.

CONTENTS

Preface

When you look in to Creich, you will find, in the first instance, a list of words creating a kind of revue (sic) of a landscape as contained in the names of places and watercourses in the parish.

This may conjure up many pictures while you read of pastoral subjects interpreted accorded to Gaelic idiom, as well as colours, sights & sounds of the countryside, and flora and fauna.

It will be possible for the reader to embark on a treasure hunt overseeing this extensive area, which is the largest parish in Scotland.

Random Gaelic Words often Found in Placenames

Baile- township	leamhan - elm	caorann - rowan	beith - birch
Fèidh - deer	ghiubhais - fir	seileach - willow	feàrna - alder
A'chuil – a nook	fuaran – well or spring	àth - ford	bàn – white bàna (plural)
Innis – meadow/pasture	lòn fliuch – wet meadow	cuithe - snowdrift	bog – soft or marshy land
abhainn - river	achadh - field	allt – stream or burn	beinn - mountain
Puill/poll – pit or muddy hole	rèidh – plain or clearing	blàr - plain	càdh – a pass
Sobhraich primrose	caor - sheep	caorach – sheep plural	cuach – cup/quaich shape
Cnoc – hill or knoll	clach aoil - limestone	creag - rock	creaganach – rocky place
Feadaig – plover	Feadain - rivulet	fraoch - heather	Fir - eòin also iolaire- eagle
Buidhe - yellow	liath - grey	glas – grey/green	fionn – white

tionnail – gathering place	teamhair - pleasant	ceap – tree roots, stumps	fàid – a long turf, a peat
Srath – a strath	na h-uidh - of the stream, or current	na h-àth – of the kiln	coire – a dell, a deep hollow often surrounded by hills.
conbhairean – dog-handler	cuinneag – small milk pail/pitcher	faichd – den/hiding place	breac – speckled
dail – dale, from O.Norse dalr	cuailean – curl, coil	beag - little	clach a'charra – standing stone
Sleagh – spear	cathraichean – chairs	sàil – heel	tuir – tower
ruathair – skirmish	odhar – dun (colour)	leacach – (of) flat stones in river-bed	creamh – garlic
leac – flagstone	tigh – house	fliuch – wet	fitheach – raven
Am bealach – the pass	An stùchd – a projecting rock	An sròn – a peak resembling a nose	aonach – barren terrain
choire bhuig – of a soft hollow	sagairt – priest	alltan – little burn	dubh – black/dark

féith – swamp or flow country	faing – fank or sheep pens	plathad – place of sudden squalls	bad daraich – oak grove, thicket
Sgàile – shady (place)	a'mheanbh – a small insect, midge	laogh – calf	Leathad – slope, hillside
Eas – waterfall	eilean – island	eòrna – barley	lìon, also lèan – flax
creagan daraich – rocks with oaks growing in clefts	tuiteam tarbhach heavy fall as in battle in year 1400	a'Charsla – river Cassley	mòinteach – peat moss, moorland
cumhainn – narrow	gleann - glen	inbhir – river-mouth	òba – creek, bay
mhadaidh – wolf	mèann – kid (goat)	muc – pig	meall – rounded hill
ceann – end	tobar – a well	bhùiridh – rutting, roaring, of stags	sgeireach – rocky
cluas – ear	tosgaire – messenger	ceàrdaich – smithy	chapuill – mare

eich – horse	miodar – pasture	càrn – a sizeable hill	eòin - birds
Bò maol – polled, hornless cow	clais mhòr – a big hollow (here) ¼ mile breadth	sgreamhaidh – heath covered rock (dangerous)	sionnach – fox
bò – cow	cladh – burial place	dubh coille – black (dark) forest	cnoc fionn – fair hill
cladh a' chnocain – a burial place on hillside	brochan – gruel	biathainne – earth worm	cliabh – creel
nam braithrean – of the brothers	sròn a'chroiche – (projecting) snout of the gallows	gamhna – stirks, one year old calves.	cròice – of antlers
cearc, circe – hen, of a hen	garbh – rough	caonnag – a fight	lùb – bend of a river.

Introduction

When Bonar Bridge Local History Society agreed on a topic for the 2005 Major Project it became clear that toponymy (study of place names) would be the favoured choice since there were no place names recorded before 1000 AD.

Examination of ancient maps along with a wealth of local knowledge, gathered over the years, were the deciding factors in writing the book from a Gaelic perspective.

Creich Parish in the County of Sutherland, the chosen area of study for our purpose, is the largest in Scotland and includes Bonar Bridge, the major settlement in the parish.

The purpose here is to document this important part of our heritage, reminding the reader of the origin of the Gaelic place names, descriptive of physical geography surrounding us at all times.
It is obvious that when Gaelic ceased to be the linguistic medium of communication and Standard English replaced it, place names gradually changed.

Glaciers and water have been the sculptors of the Highland landscape, inspiring early Gaelic writers to produce poetry of considerable artistic merit.

The origin of Gaelic is derived from one of the Indo-European languages of which there are many branches and sub-branches. Here we have to watch our Ps and Qs because they have more relevance to language than we are aware, taking into account that Gaelic is in the Goidelic category called Q-Celtic. And in the Scottish Highlands the term is Gàidhlig.

As in other early cultures, knowledge was carried in people's memories, but here, the content has come from the findings of academic study as well as through the oral tradition. Up to the time of the Reformation, in the 17th century Irish and Scottish Gaelic had a common literary language, although the spoken tongues had diverged. The Gaelic alphabet consists of eighteen letters, namely, a, b, c, d, e, f, g, h, i, l, m, n, o, p, r, s, t, u. as used in modern Gaelic.
Several MSS were written in the 11th and 12th centuries but the first printed literature in Scottish Gaelic dates from 1567,when the Earl of Argyll commissioned the author John Carswell, to issue a translation of John Knox's Liturgy.
A manuscript written in Scottish Gaelic, known as The Book of Deer, is the oldest document written in O.G. (a phonetic link with Scottish Gaelic)
The above is a view held by the late Dr MacBain. Entries in the document were made in the 11th and 12th centuries, the most important being the first, named the Legend of Deer extending to nineteen lines of continuous prose

Gaelic was spoken extensively at the time of the Battle of Carham, in 1018, "when it ran from Tweed and Solway to the Pentland Firth, but by 1530 Scots living along the Border had forsaken the mother-tongue"-as said by Professor W.J Watson.

The daunting task of attempting to summarise ancient history within a given compass has proved to be a difficult one, especially in the absence of written evidence to confirm accurate boundaries applicable to the extent of the Pictish kingdom.

In the 12th century the author of De Situe Albania identified seven Pictish Provinces in Scotland, each held by a King under whom, ruled a petty king or sub-regulus. Provincial kings became Mormaers who were the high stewards and, in turn became Earls and later still the title of Duke came into existence. The institution of Thane was originally designated as a royal official responsible for Royal estates.

The Pictish practice of twinning names for governmental purposes applied to the Province of Cait, now the parliamentary constituency of Caithness & Sutherland. Incidentally our serving Member of Parliament is indeed a descendant of a Norse Earl of Caithness, the earldom having been granted to the Sinclairs at the same time as the earldom of Sutherland was ceded to the county of Sutherland.

It is documented that a Norse earl ruled the Pictish province of Cait for a time, through the agency of the Scottish Crown thus explaining the legacy of Norse names, particularly in Caithness.

Our aim in publishing this book is to provide information for the student who may not be familiar with Gaelic language and culture. It is helpful also to grasp how certain events in history changed society and developed the use of the indigenous language. This is illustrated throughout the book when it is seen that much has been learned from the historic migration of peoples over the centuries.

We have listened to informed opinion on languages and on history and hope that what is now written will be of interest, and lead to further research by the reader for his or her pleasure.

Of necessity, we have to go back a long way in history, by learning from history books that in 789 AD King Constantine 1 was king of all the Pictish provinces and that by 811, he was also king of Argyll.
In that same year he travelled, with Gaelic-speaking monks from Argyll, to the eastern side of the country developing and spreading the language.

It is important to note at this point that in 794, Viking invaders attacked the Northern and Western Isles repeatedly plundering the Isle of Iona, which by 806 resulted in the slaughter of sixty-eight monks on that island.

In the year 839 the Pictish king, his sons, and his noblemen were annihilated during raids by the Scandinavians, who were operating from their bases in Orkney and Shetland. At that time the Norwegians were known as Fionnghaill, meaning the fair strangers while the Danes were called Dubhghaill, the dark strangers.

The new King of Scots, Kenneth MacAlpin, asserted his rights in 843 by establishing the primacy of the Gaelic language in the greater part of the country, when the kingdom became known as Alba.
The name Scotia, derived from Latin, was used by non-gaels, similarly the name Scotti, referring to the Q-Celtic people, who came from Ireland, also had Latin origins.

In 1070 when the Scots ruling monarch Malcolm III married Margaret, princess of the ancient royal House of Wessex, they had six sons all of whom were given English titles changing the continuum of Gaelic names for future kings.

Until the late 11th century Gaelic was still the dominant language, but the accession of King David I (1124-53) brought an historical change, creating a new sense of identity among the different peoples of Scotland heralding a period of political, economic and linguistic development.

Derivation of Creich

From 1230 there have been various spellings for the parish territory, which stretches for over 30 miles from east to west.

Research has shown the following variations in spelling:

In 1230 - Crech, 1275 - Creych, 1562 - Criech, 1556 - Criech 1569 - Creich

In November 1874 a letter signed by one, John Maclean, was sent to Ordnance Survey Office stating that the English spelling - CREICH- should be adopted. The Gaelic word is Crìche, genitive of Crioche meaning boundary.

In 1569 Donald Logan was appointed "reider in the Irsihe Tonng."

The parish had been ecclesiastically formed in 1225, after which the church gave it the name of Creich. Researchers have found that the name came from a rock known in Caledonian – Pictish times as Din-Crûg a word meaning a place of striking visual impact.

The rocky headland is now known as Dùn Creich.

The main purpose in producing this work is to list and preserve the Gaelic place names represented on Ordnance Survey maps, Sheets 13 and 21.

The Parish of Creich in the County of Sutherland is no longer a Gaelic-speaking community.

To understand how a place acquired a name takes us to the root of the matter. Obsolete words from other cultures may be the etymon of a word, but would not be helpful in orienteering. When travelling, it has always been useful to have a place name to avoid becoming lost, so in the past, observation and description of landmarks would have provided guidance before there was a method of recording place names and signage as known today.

Before roads existed and when the land was covered with thick natural forest, mainly of oak and birch, two forts were built to guard the waterway now known as the Dornoch Firth, the reasoning being that this would be the quickest way to access a land route into the hinterland.

The hill itself rises to 370ft. above the estuary waters which link the Kyle of Sutherland with the Dornoch Firth 3½ miles SE of Bonar Bridge. It is in fact a wooded, rocky headland on which the fortification, Dùn Creich was built in the Middle Ages at the same time as Dùn Alcaig was built, immediately opposite, on the south side of the waterway.

For many years the navigable channel facilitated a sea route for a distance of 10 miles beyond the present bridge at Bonar. Considerable traffic plied the water exporting and importing goods.

It is hoped that the book titled "Looking in to Creich" will be a useful contribution to the Highland Year of Culture 2007.

In general we keep to local historic facts beginning with the extent of the parish, ignoring recent designated boundaries created for electoral reasons.

The 33 mile long territory extending from Rivaig which marks the eastern boundary with the neighbouring Parish of Dornoch, to the western march with the Parish of Assynt which point is at Dubh Loch Mòr not far from the base of the highest mountain in the County of Sutherland, rising to a height of 3273 ft. and known as Ben More Assynt (Beinn Mhòr Assainte). The place name is derived from Gaelic and Norse.

The neighbouring parishes to the North are Rogart and Lairg, while the Kyle of Sutherland marks the southern boundary with the Parish of Kincardine in the County of Ross. The word Kyle is a corrupted Gaelic one - caolas - meaning a strait or a sound in geographic terms.

According to 1874 records examined along with the 19th century statistical account, the Kyle of Sutherland average length is ten miles and is described as a tidal stream from the confluence of the rivers Cassley and Oykel (both Norse names) after which it takes the name of the Dornoch Firth and gives the name Portnaculter to a place known today as Meikle Ferry, in operational terms a misnomer.

The principal landowners of the parish at that time were the Duke of Sutherland at Dunrobin Castle, E. Sutherland Walker at Skibo, Sir Charles Ross at Balnagowan Castle Ross-shire and G.G. Mackay Esq., Rosehall.

The Earldom of Sutherland was created in the 13th century for a branch of a Norman family of Freskyn, passing through an heiress to a branch of the Gordons.

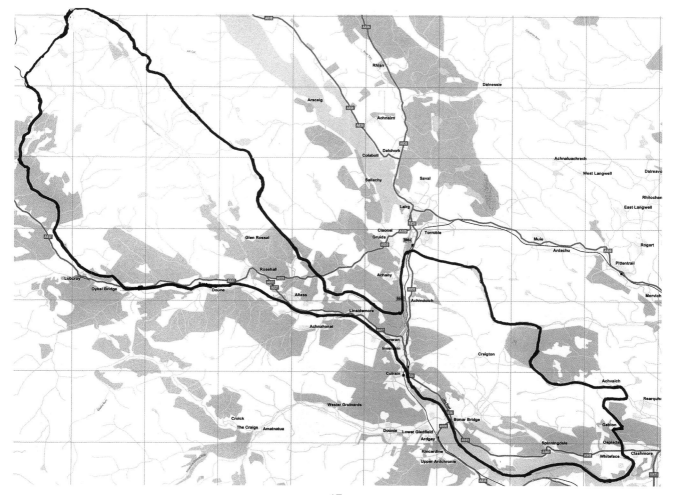

17

Place Names from Dornoch Boundary to River Shin
(Using Ordnance Survey references)
Key: **O** = origin   **G** = Gaelic   **P** = Pictish
ON = Old Norse   **N** = Norse

Grid Ref	Gaelic Name	O	Common Name	Interpretation/ Literal Translation	Comment
NH 677 954	Abhainn an t-Strath Chàrnaig	G	Strath Carnaig		A river flowing from Loch Buidhe (675 984) running through Strath Carnaig to Dail na Mèinne, thence into R. Evelix
NH 673 915	Achaidh	G		Obsolete word	As Achadh, place of fields
NH 708 897	Ach Àirigh or Achadh a' Charragh	G	Acharry	Field of the standing stone most likely	From (1) field of the shieling or (2) achadh+carradh becoming Achadh a'Charragh
NH 682 914	Ach a'Bhad Sgàile	G	Achbadsgaile	The field of the shady thicket	A settlement of 5 houses

Grid Ref	Gaelic Name	O	Common Name	Interpretation/ Literal Translation	Comment
NH 713 942	Ach a' Bhàthaiche	G	Achvaich	Field of the byre	
NH 666 895	A'Chraisg	G	Crask		A hill W of Spinningdale
NH 581 011	Ach an dubhach	G	Achinduich		Field of gloom or sorrow?
NH 515 999	Ach an t-Sabhal	G	Achintoul	Field of the barn	
NH 694 948	Achormlary				No information
NH 673 914	Achu	G			Derivative of Achadh (field)
NH 622 953	An t-Achadh Uaine	G	Achuaine	The green field	

19

Grid Ref	Gaelic Name	O	Common Name	Interpretation/ Literal Translation	Comment
NH 630 943	A' Chùil	G	Achuil	The nook	A sheltered croft NW of Airdens
NH 635 935	Achadh torr fala	G	Achtorfale	The field of the rocky hillock of blood	A croft with turf enclosure, possibly where cattle were bled
NH 620 935	Àirdean	G	Airdens district	The high places	A good example of efficient crofting
NH 627 956	Astail	G/N +ON	Asdle/Ausdale	A dwelling in Gaelic	From dalr (east)
NH 701 906	A'Chreagach A'chreaganach	G		The rocky place	1 1/2mile NW of Ospisdale
NH 649 929	Allt na h-àtha	G		Burn of the ford/kiln	The kiln burn – running into Migdale burn

Grid Ref	Gaelic Name	O	Common Name	Interpretation/ Literal Translation	Comment
NH 603 974	Allt na Ciste Dubh	G	Hen man's burn - recent folk lore	Stream of the black chest/coffin	Source at an t'Seillach. Flows E .to W. into R Shin
NH	Allt na Claise Mòire	G		Stream of the big hollow	Source NE of Cnoc Tionail flowing into Kyle of Sutherland forming a boundary between Maikle and Balblair woods
NH	Allt Clais an Fhuarain	G		The burn of the cleft of the spring	A stream issuing from Loch a'Ghiuthais, flowing NW.to River Evelix
NH	Allt Coire nan Caorach	G		Stream of the corrie of the sheep (grazing)	Main stream on the E side of Cnòc Dubh Mòr flowing into the Dornoch Firth.
NH 625 925	Alltan Dubh	G		Little black stream	
NH 628 925	Allt na Garbh àiridh	G	Garvary burn	Stream of the rough pasture	Flows into Loch Buidhe.The word airigh means shieling.

Grid Ref	Gaelic Name	O	Common Name	Interpretation/ Literal Translation	Comment
NH	Allt na Gòiste	G		Stream of the snare/trap	Source in hill –(An) Sìthean flows SW, into Kyle of Sutherland at Invershin
NH	Allt Loch Làrach	G	Loch Laro	Làraich. Old Celtic word for mares	Stream flows SE to join Loch Leisgean
NH	Allt Loch Losgann	G	Loch Leisgeinn	Stream of the loch of frogs	Source NW of Cnòc Dubh flows NE.into Locha' Gabhaire
NH	Allt Mòr	G	Altmore	Big stream	Name changes to Alltan Loch Duibh at Ceannabhaid flows SW. through Airdens falling into Migdale Burn
NH	Allt Rèidhe Dhorcha	G		Stream of the dark plain	Flows S. into R.Shin ¾ mile from N.of Shin river
NH	Allt Rèidh nam Mèann	G	Rhinamain	Burn of the plain of the kids (goats)	Source in Cnòc Coire Buidhe NH 611 955
NH	Allt na Seann àiridh	G	Shennary	Burn of the old shieling (disused)	Source Loch Lagain, A Creich/Dornoch boundary and flowing into R. Evelix

22

Grid Ref	Gaelic Name	O	Common Name	Interpretation/ Literal Translation	Comment
NH 630 934	Bad a'Chùil	G		Thicket of the nook	Two crofts and a clump of trees
NH 637 914	Bad Beith	G	Badbay	Birch grove	A place of several crofts among trees on N. side of Loch Migdale
NH 632 961	Am bad Bog	G	Badbog	The soft thicket	A soft place, boggy.
NH 639 938	Bad na Cuach	G		A clump of trees with birds' nests	Cuach means a bowl shape of a nest
NH 642 881	Am Bad Darach	G		The oak thicket	On shore S. of Creich House
NH 641 947	Am Badan Guineach	G		The sharp little thicket	A clump of thorny trees or shrubs
NH 580 950	Baile na Creagan	G	Balchraggan	Rocky township	

Grid Ref	Gaelic Name	O	Common Name	Interpretation/ Literal Translation	Comment
NH 682 898	Baile na Croite	G		Township of the croft	A crofting district E.of Spinningdale
NH 675 903	Baile na Cùil	G		Township of the nook	A sheltered situation
NH 677 900	Baile nan Alltan	G	Balanaltan	Township of small burns	
NH 591 944	Baile a'Bhlàir	G	Balblair	Township of the plain	
NH	Baile an Droma?	G	Baldruim wood	Township of the ridge	Droman in Gaelic little hill or ridge
NH 713 915	Baile na Beinne			High township	Shown on map as Bardnabeinne - suggested meaning of bard is a dyke enclosure allocated to the Chief (of the clan)
NH 629 924	Baile na Craobh	G	Balnagrew	Township of the tree	

Grid Ref	Gaelic Name	O	Common Name	Interpretation/ Literal Translation	Comment
NH 635 915	Breacwell	G N		Speckled field	2 crofts above Loch Migdale
NH 705 935	Am Blàr Odhar	G		The dun coloured plain	Dwellings on W.side of Acharry Moor
NH 634 936	Blàr Lòn Lochan a' Ghobair	G		Plain of the marsh of the small loch of the goat	
NH 635 942			Campbelton		Croft NE of Airdens
NH 622 922	Càrn nam Fitheach	G	Tulloch Hill	Hill of the raven	Site of the find (1900) named the Migdale Hoard
NH 682 916	Càrn Dubh	G		Black cairn	A crofting area
NH 637 938	Ceann a' Bhaid	G	Ceannabad	End of the thicket	

Grid Ref	Gaelic Name	O	Common Name	Interpretation/ Literal Translation	Comment
NH 625 918	Ceann an locha	G	Lochend	At the end of the loch	Croft at W end of Loch Migdale
NH 666 954	Ceann Loch Lagain	G	Kinlochlaggan	At the end of the loch in the hollow	
NH 625 965	Ceann a'Chreag	G	Craigton	Head of the rock	
NH 719 896	Clach a'Charra	G	Standing stone	From carragh meaning erect stone or monument	Legend: Danish Chief slain by laird of Pulrossie Fact: human remains and Norse brooch found 1830 The stone is a memorial to a Norse commander, Hospis who was killed in defeat in the 11th century
NH	A'Chlach Dhubh	G		The black stone (on foreshore E of Spinningdale)	Situated on foreshore east of Spinningdale

Grid Ref	Gaelic Name	O	Common Name	Interpretation/ Literal Translation	Comment
NH 660 890	A'Chlach Shleamhainn	G		The slippery stone	Situated W of Spinningdale
NH 639 939	A'Chlais Coig	G	Clashcoig	1/5th is a land division. Coig = 5	Here, situated in a hollow, the work trench or a cutting.
NH 641 963	A'Chlais Bhàn	G	Clashbaan	The fair cutting or furrow	
NH 689 911	Na Claisean Glas(a)	G	Claiseanglas Sounding like clashinglas	A grey furrows	The grey/green cuttings. In Old Gaelic, glas means green
NH 690 905	Clais nam Fàd	G		A peat bank	
NH 635 939	A'Chlais Bhuidhe	G		Yellow hollow	Asphodels growing here
NH 635 976	Clais na Sionnach	G		Hollow of the fox	Situated at the foot of Sìthean Mòr, see reference

Grid Ref	Gaelic Name	O	Common Name	Interpretation/ Literal Translation	Comment
NH 680 928	Clais na Prontonnach	G			Shepherd's dwelling here N of Claiseanglas
NH 682 952	Clais na Cuinneag	G		Trench of the wooden milk pails	Possibly a shieling nearby
NH 590 031	Cnoc an Achaidh Mhòire	G		The big hill of the field	
NH 593 981	Cnoc Breac	G		The speckled hill	756ft
NH 609 956	Cnoc a' Choire Bhuidhe	G		Hill of the yellow corrie	975 ft.
NH 685 905	Cnoc a'Chapuill	G		Hill of the horse/mare	A hill S of Claiseanglas
NH 701 953	Cnoc na Feadaig	G		Hill of the plover	

Grid Ref	Gaelic Name	O	Common Name	Interpretation/ Literal Translation	Comment
NH 639 918	Cnoc na Mòine	G		Hill of the peat moss	898 ft.
NH	Creag na Cloich Aoil	G		Rock of the limestone	A small community of crofts
NH 659 921	Creag A'Bhealaich	G		Rock of the pass	A crag (1890 ft) 2 miles E of Migdale, above Kyloag
NH 632 942	Na Creagan Reamhar	G		A small rocky hill of conical shape. 633ft.	Reamhar- a gaelic word for fat. Here refers to circumference.
NH 640 083	Coill a'Bhaid Daraich	G		The wood of the oak thicket	Oak wood south of Creich House
NH 704 895	Coille an Rèidh Mhòir	G	Rimore forest	The wood of the big plain	
NH 685 894	Coille Baile na Creag	G		The wood of the township of the rock	S.of Bailenacroite Spinningdale

Grid Ref	Gaelic Name	O	Common Name	Interpretation/ Literal Translation	Comment
NH 695 895	Coille nan Creagan Ruadh	G		The wood of the russet rocks	Spinningdale
NH 661 910	Coille Òg	G	Kyleoag	Young forest	Near Spinningdale
NH 676 905	Coille Baile na Cùil	G	Back town wood	Forest in the township of the sheltered corner	A short distance N.of Spinningdale on the road to Kyleoag at (661 910)
NH 659 921	Creag a' Bhealaich	G		The rock of the pass	A crag (1098ft) N. of Kyleoag 2miles E. of Migdale
NH 659 941	Creag a'Ghobhair	G		The rock of the goat	3 ¼ miles NE.of Bonar Bridge
	Creag Liath	G		Small hill of grey rock	NE of Spinningdale
NH 646 937	Creag na Faire	G		The view rock	A 266ft. hill NE of Migdale
NH 668 893	Creag na Sròine	G		The rock of the nose	A promontory west of Spinningdale

Grid Ref	Gaelic Name	O	Common Name	Interpretation/ Literal Translation	Comment
NH	Creag an Fhithich	G		The rock of the raven	1mile E of Spinningdale
NH 691 940	An Dail Bhreac	G/ N		The speckled dale	NW of Ospisdale stoney ground. Dail in Scots is Haugh
NH 611 918	Drochaid a' Bhàn-àth	G	Bonar Bridge	Bridge at the end/bottom of the ford	In 1275 OG form Bunnach. Later Bun-aw meaning mouth of river, aw now an obsolete Caledonian-Pictish word for running water. In modern Gaelic àth meaning shallow running water, as a ford, in this case, tidal water.
NH 643 956	Drochaid an Fhèidh	G		The bridge of the deer	Re-named. See below

Grid Ref	Gaelic Name	O	Common Name	Interpretation/ Literal Translation	Comment
NH 643 936	Drochaid na h-ù idh	G	Ùidh common usage in Sutherland	Bridge of the slow burn.	A slow running burn connecting two lochs
NH 625 935	Druim Bàn	G	Drumban	White ridge	Poor or bare land
NH 615 932	An Druim Liath	G	Drumliath	The grey ridge	In the district of Tulloch
NH 639 938	Druim Taighe	G	Drumtighe	House ridge	A ridge near the house
NH 651 882	Dùn Creich	G	Dun of Creich	Fortress at Creich	Remains of Iron age fort and of Medieval castle 370ft. in height, affording magnificent views
NH 685 904	An Fhèith Bhuidhe	G		The yellow bog	Swamp area, in modern English language, flow country (channels)
NH	An Fhèith Mòr	G		The big bog	Flow country

Grid Ref	Gaelic Name	O	Common Name	Interpretation/ Literal Translation	Comment
NH 708 887	Flode	N	Fload	Flat place	A farm north of Newton Point
NH 715 915	Gablon				A small settlement
NH 633 933	Garbh àiridh	G	Garvary	The rough shieling	A high croft close to the Rogart Parish boundary
NH 610 942	Garbh Leathad	G	Gurlet	The rough slope	A few small crofts 1.5 miles N.W. of Bonar
NH 694 982	Leathad a'Chaorann	G		Slope of the rowan	
NH 657 964	Leathad a'Chuailein	G		Slope of the swirls or coils	Interpretation suggests snow wreaths, in view of location. A 200ft hill
NH 655 950	Leathad na Caora	G		Slope of the sheep	On the S. side of Loch Lagain
NH 696	Loch Saine			Hill Loch	West of Acharry

Grid Ref	Gaelic Name	O	Common Name	Interpretation/ Literal Translation	Comment
NH 635 905	Leathad an Locha	G		Slope of the loch	On the south side of Loch Migdale
NH 665 893	Leathad Mòr	G	Ledmore	Big slope	Natural forest
NH 611 954	Leathad Sòbhraich	G	Lydsurich	Slope abounding in primroses	3 crofts near N side of Maikle wood
NH 685 935	Leathad Seileach	G	Lydsuileach	Willow slope	Wrong spelling on map.
NH 665 985	Loch Bhuidhe	G	Loch Buie five miles N of Bonar	Yellow loch, reflecting the moorland colour	Centre of loch represents the N parish boundary
NH 630 005	Loch Cracail Beag and Loch Cracail Mòr (625 020)		Loch crykel	One small, and one large loch	In Gaelic, cracail means cracking. Location is on high land near Cnoc Cracail, - suggesting frost and the cracking of ice.

Grid Ref	Gaelic Name	O	Common Name	Interpretation/ Literal Translation	Comment
NH 669 925	Loch Coire nan Ceap	G		Loch of the corrie (a circular hollow surrounded by hills) of ceap-tree stumps	In Gaelic ceap means turf as well as tree stumps or roots.
NH 605 995		N	Loch Laro		Original spelling was Làraich from Old Celtic meaning – mares.
NH 652 957	Loch Lagain		Loch Laggan	Loch of the little hollow	Loch in a hollow
NH 665 930	Loch Losgann	G		Loch of toads or frogs	
NH 655 935	Loch a'Gobhair	G		Goats' loch	
NH 687 921	Loch nan Gillean	G		Ostensibly the loch of the young men.	More likely originally Loch nan Gilean, a loch fed by waters from gullies or watercourses

Grid Ref	Gaelic Name	O	Common Name	Interpretation/ Literal Translation	Comment
NH 711 930	Loch a'Ghiùthais	G		Loch of the fir trees.	On the S. shore, a Creich /Dornoch boundary
NC 366 026	Lochan nan Smugaidean	G		Little loch of the spits	"Cuckoo spittle"
NH 701 903	An Loch as àirde	G		The highest loch	
NH 621 963	Lòn a'Bhothain	G		The meadow of the bothy or cottage	
NH 718 939	An Lòn Fliuch	G		The wet meadow	Lòn indicates marshy land
NH 642 922	Lòn a'Ghiùthais	G	Longuish	The meadow of the pine	
	Lòn nan Searrach	G	Lonansearrach	The meadow of the foals	Near Claiseanglas

Grid Ref	Gaelic Name	O	Common Name	Interpretation/ Literal Translation	Comment
NH 593 398	Maikle	N? G?			If from Gaelic meigeal, meaning bleating of goats which is quite feasible since it is just over the hill from Rèidh nam Meann (plain of the kids)
NH 658 968	Meall Mòr	G		The big hill	South of Loch Buidhe
NH 664 942	Meall Morag	G		A personal name	3 ¾ M. NE of Bonar Bridge
NH 665 947	Meall na Diollaid	G		Hill of the saddle	
NH 595 962	Mòine Bhuidhe	G		The yellow peat moss	Landscape natural colour Asphodel plants grow here.
NH 693 922	A'Mhòine Dhaor	G			A district of small crofts. The word daor means expensive, leading to the belief that peat harvesting would be difficult. .

Grid Ref	Gaelic Name	O	Common Name	Interpretation/ Literal Translation	Comment
NH 712 897	Ospisdale	N			A Norse personal name, Opis
NH 675 895	Am Poll Mòraichte	G		The enlarged pool	At mouth of Spinningdale burn
NH 619 989	Puill Fhraoich	G		Heath clad peat bank, muddy area	Poll may mean, according to application, a sea inlet, a river pool or a peat bank.
NH 725 884	Pulrossie	G/ N		Hross meaning horse is the Norse part of the literal translation- muddy bog or pit of the horse.	If the first part is Gaelic the correct spelling would be pollhross
NH 635 964	An Rèidhe Breac	G	Reidhbreck	The Speckled plain	

Grid Ref	Gaelic Name	O	Common Name	Interpretation/ Literal Translation	Comment
NH 618 931	Rèidh nam Mèann	G	Rhinamain	The plain of the kids (goats)	
NH 725 895	Rhi-beag	G	Riavaig as on O.S. map	Rhi beag means small downward slope	Here is the E Parish boundary neighbouring with the Parish of Dornoch
NH 671 907		N	Rhivra		
NH 623 938	Seana Bhaile	G	Shennaval	Old township	A croft in Airdens District
NH 674 898	Spinningdale	N		The attractive dale	From Spenja-Attractive and Dalr- dale
NH 615 905	Swordale	N		The green sward dale	Svordr-sward, and dalr- dale

Grid Ref	Gaelic Name	O	Common Name	Interpretation/ Literal Translation	Comment
NH 643 976	Salachaidh	G	Salachy	Place of willows	
NH 690 911	Sithean Dearg Beag	G		The little (red) fairy hill	Situated NE of Migdale
NH 694 913	Sithean Dearg Mòr	G		The big (red) fairy hill	Red is descriptive of the colour of the soil
NH 644 964	Sleasdairidh	G	Sleastary	Sleast àiraidh	The dirty shieling possibly because it was the place where cattle and sheep had horns marked.
NH 615 985	Sròn Ach a'Bhàcaidh	G	Stronavachy	The nose of the field of the hindrance	An area 928ft high, which is difficult terrain for walking.
NH 625 925	Tulloch Hill (District)	G		184ft.hill derivation- Tulach - a hillock.	Site of many burial cairns and site of a Battle in 1031

Grid Ref	Gaelic Name	O	Common Name	Interpretation/ Literal Translation	Comment
NC 365 187	Allt a'Chnaip Ghiuthais	G		Burn of the pine cone - fir trees	A big stream rising in Ben More Assynt flowing into R. Cassley
NC 434 020	Allt a'Chnocain	G		Burn on the little hill	A big stream flowing SE into R. Oykel east of Tutim
NC	Allt a'Choire Bhuidhe	G	Corbuie	the yellow hollow	A stream rising in Corbuie flowing SW to join Allt Drughaidh Beag ½ mile from the R. Oykel
NC	Allt a'Choire Bhuig	G		Burn of the soft hollow	A stream rising in Coire Bog flowing through Bad Mòr into R. Cassley to Lùb Bad na h- Ula
NC 364 080	Allt a' Choire Dhuibh	G		Burn of the dark hollow	A big stream flowing W out of Coir Dubh into Allt Drughaid Mòr

Grid Ref	Gaelic Name	O	Common Name	Interpretation/ Literal Translation	Comment
NC	Allt a'Ghlas Choille	G		Burn of the grey wood	A big stream flowing into R.Cassley
NC 390 129	Allt a' Mheanbh Bhith	G		Burn of the small creature	A stream flowing NE into Abhainn Gleann na Muic
NC 320 160	Allt an Dubh Loch Beag	G		Burn of the little dark loch	A small stream flowing SW out of Dubh Loch Beag into R,Oykel
NC	Allt an Dubh Loch Mhòir	G		Burn of the big black loch	A stream flowing SW to its confluence with Allt an Dubh Loch Bhig after which it is called Allt Langwell,entering R.Cassley
Nc	Allt Dubh Loch Bhig	G		Burn of the little black loch	A small stream flowing out of Dubh Loch Bhig to join Allt an Dubh Mhòr
NC 310 183	Allt an Dubh Loch Mòr	G		Burn of the big dark loch	A big stream flowing SW from Dubh Loch Mòr into R.Oykel

Grid Ref	Gaelic Name	O	Common Name	Interpretation/ Literal Translation	Comment
NC 324 153	Allt an Fhaing	G	fank -Scots word	Burn of the fank or sheep pens	A mountain stream flowing into R.Oykel not far from N of Cnoc Fionn
NC 455 063	Allt an Rasail	G N	Hross-Vollr	Burn of the horse field	A big stream flowing from Loch an Rasail into R.Cassley 1 ¼ mls.SE of Glencassley
NC 455 032	Allt an Tuir	G		Burn of the tower	No evidence of tower visible- a stream flowing into R.Cassley
NC 440 088	Allt Bad a'Chreamh	G		Burn of the thicket of garlic	A little stream flowing W to R.Cassley ¾ mile from NNW of Glencassley Castle
NC 407 051	Allt Bad air Dhonnadh	G	Batrighonie	Burn of the browned grove	A big stream rising in Clais Mòr and called Allt na Claise Mòire for half its length, then receiving tributaries when it is known as Allt Bad air Dhonnadh falling into R.Oykel

Grid Ref	Gaelic Name	O	Common Name	Interpretation/ Literal Translation	Comment
NC 435 103	Allt Bad an t-Sagairt	G		Burn of the priest's grove	A big stream flowing W into R.Cassley ¼ ml.from Badintagairt
NH 435 972	Allt Beinn an Rasail	G N	Hross-vollr	Burn of the horse field	A little stream flowing E into R.Cassley
NC 410 107	Allt Càrn a' Chòta	G		Burn of the hill (summit?) of the coat	A stream Rising in Càrn a' Chòta flowing NW into R.Cassley
NC 405 113	Allt Càrn a' Ceàrdaich	G		Burn of the cairn of the smithy	A stream flowing NE falling into R.Cassley
NC	Allt Choire Ghlas	G		Burn of the grey hollow.	A stream flowing SW into Allt Drughaidh Mor ½ mile N Allt a'Choire Dhuibh
NC	Allt Dail Fòid	G		Burn of the peat plain (moss)	A stream rising in the watershed flowing into R.Cassley, midway between Dalnaclave and Duchally
NC	Allt Clais an Fhuarain	G		Burn of the cleft of the spring	

Grid Ref	Gaelic Name	O	Common Name	Interpretation/ Literal Translation	Comment
NC	Allt Dail Teamhair	G		Burn of the pleasant plain	A stream out of a lochan flowing into the R.Cassley
NC 350 052	Allt Drughaid Beag	G		Little oozing (draining) burn	A stream flowing W from Loch na Claise Mòire into R.Oykel NW of Caplich
NC 350 063	Allt Drughaid Mòr	G		Big oozing (draining) burn	A stream draining into R.Oykel ½ mile.below Salachy
NC 445 080	Allt Innis na Circe	G		Burn of the pasture of the hen. Gaelic for moor-hen is cearc.	A stream flowing W into R,Cassley ½ mile NW of Glencassley Castle
NC	Allt Langwell	G N		If pure Norse, spelling would be Langwelldale	A big stream formed by the confluence of Allt an Dubh Loch Bhig and Allt an Dubh Loch Mòr
HC 3701 78	Allt Loch Càrn nan Conbhairean	G		Burn of the loch of the hill of the kennel boys. Conbhair =hunting dog handler.	A big stream from the loch flowing into R.Cassley in Glen Cassley

Grid Ref	Gaelic Name	O	Common Name	Interpretation/ Literal Translation	Comment
NC 3251 03	Allt na Cailliche	G		Burn of the old woman	A stream flowing out of Loch Meall a'Bhuiridh falling into Loch Ailsh
NC	Allt na Claise Mòire	G		Burn of the big hollow	A big stream flowing into R.Oykel 3ml. SE of Oykel Bridge
NC	Allt na Crìche	G		Burn of the boundary	1/4 mile W of Aonacha'Choire Bhuig flowing into R.Cassley ½ ml. NW of Lùb Bad na h- Ula
NC 4200 99	Allt na Cròice	G		Burn of the antler	A big stream flowing NE into R.Cassley at Croick settlement
NC 4300 80	Allt na Faichde	G		Name as loch Faichde loch of the den	A stream flowing out of Loch Faichde and falling into R.Cassley near Glencassley Castle
NC 400 138	Allt na Gaibhre	G		Burn of the goat	A stream flowing into R.Cassley At Eas an Gaibhre

Grid Ref	Gaelic Name	O	Common Name	Interpretation/ Literal Translation	Comment
NC 377 016	Allt na h- Innse Beith	G		Burn of the birch valley	A stream flowing S into R.Oykel at Innse Beithe
NC 330 124	Allt nan Cathraichean Bàna	G		Burn of the fair chairs possibly white rocks used as resting places.	A stream flowing SW into R.Oykel 1/4 mile above Loch Ailsh possibly white rock where hunters would rest
NC 323 097	Allt nan Sleagh	G		Burn of the spears	A stream flowing SW into R.Oykel near Loch Ailsh
NC 333 135	Allt Sàil an Ruathair	G		Burn of the heel of the skirmish	A stream flowing SW from small loch,into R.Oykel 1mile above Loch Ailsh
NC 356 155	Allt Sròn Sgàile	G		Burn of the shadowy hill - a promontory. sròn =nose	A stream flowing S into the head of Glen Muic after which its name is Abhainn Gleann Muic

Grid Ref	Gaelic Name	O	Common Name	Interpretation/ Literal Translation	Comment
NC 400 005	Alltan Leacach	G		Streamlet of the flat stones	A stream flowing N to near Loch Tournaig where it bends sharply round to the east, falling into R.Oykel
NC 430 108	Alltan Leacach	G		Flagstone streamlet	A stream flowing SW into Bad an t-sagairt ¼ mile NW of Badintagairt
NC 492 002	Altais Beag	G	Altassbeg	Little place of heights	
NC 500 000	Altais Mhòr	G	Altassmore	Alt = cliff or high place	
NC 302 192	Am Bealach	G		The pass	A pass across Breabag Tarsuinn, at the head of Glen Oykel, and western base of Ben More Assynt
NC 317 180	Am Plathad	G		The place of sudden squalls also a flat place	A mossy flat situated between two lochs at the NE base of Càrn a'Mhiodar

Grid Ref	Gaelic Name	O	Common Name	Interpretation/ Literal Translation	Comment
NC 390 131	Abhainn na Muic	G		River of the pig	A river going through Gleann Muic into R.Cassley
NC 341 090	An Stùchd	G		The little hill, jutting out from a bigger hill	About 2 miles. SE of Loch Ailsh
NC 385 144	An t-Sròn	G		The snout hill.	A ridge or nose of a hill 1195ft
NC 474 087	Aonach a'Choire Bhuig			A deep soft corrie	A steep heathy 1058 ft.hill partly in Lairg Parish
NC	Aonach Coire an Laogh	G		Wilderness of the corrie of the calf	A barren hill1/2 mile E of Coire an Laogh
NC 440 086	Bad a'Chuithe	G		Place of the wreath (snow)	A wooded slope of 2miles on the W side of Glen Cassley
NC 409 012	Bad Air Dhonnadh	G	Batrighonie	Browned grove	A dense wood possibly withering

Grid Ref	Gaelic Name	O	Common Name	Interpretation/ Literal Translation	Comment
NC 465 044	Bad Mòr	G		Big thicket	Chiefly birch wood on the E side of Glen Cassley
NC 428 108	Bad an t-sagairt	G	Badintagairt	Grove of the priest, a clump of trees	On the E side of Glen Cassley 7 miles above Rosehall
NC 389 083	Beinn an Eòin	G		Mountain of the birds	1785ft mountain of heath pasture about 2 miles from Croich
NC 413 066	Beinn an Rasail	G N		Mountain of the horse field	1341 ft.mountain1mile from Loch Faichde
NC 453 118	Beinn Sgeireach	G		Rocky cairn	A cairn of small rocks on the top N of Càrn nam Bò Maol
NC 441 151	Beinn Sgreamhaidh	G		Dreadful mountain	Nasty heath-covered rocky pasture (dangerous terrain?)
NH 323 115	Ben More Lodge				Hunting Lodge

Grid Ref	Gaelic Name	O	Common Name	Interpretation/ Literal Translation	Comment
NC 319 202	Beinn Mhòr Asainnte	G	Ben More Assynt	Parish name – Assynt,the map configuration has many coastline sea inlets.	The highest mountain in Sutherland 3273ft and just outside the boundary with Creich parish. Some rivers running through Creich have sources in the ben. It has been suggested that Asainte may mean out and in, describing the coastline
NC 358 086	Cadh'an Eich	G		Pass of the horses	A pass between Allt a'Choire Ghlas and Allt Drughaidh Mòr
NC 352 030	Caplich	G		Horse place, capull meaning mare	A shepherd's house here
NC 422 105	A'Chaiplich	G		The horse pasturing place	A grassy plain on the bank of the Cassley E of Croich
NC 401 085	Càrn a'Chòta	G		Cairn of the coat, the summit	A hill 1693 ft.3 mls.NE of Beinn Eoghainn

Grid Ref	Gaelic Name	O	Common Name	Interpretation/ Literal Translation	Comment
NC 319 170	Càrn a' Mhiodar	G		Cairn of the good pasture. Miodar also means wooden (milk) pail.	A high hill on the E side of Glen Oykel
NC 415 034	Càrn Beag	G		Little cairn	A small hill 808ft.1mile SE of Càrn Mòr
NC 403 445	An Càrn Mòr	G		Big cairn	A large hill 1133ft.
NC 383 098	Càrn na Ceàrdaich	G		Cairn of the smithy	A hill 1633ft. NW of Beinn Eoin
NC 453 096	Càrn nam Bò Maol	G		Cairn of the hornless cow (polled)	A little cairn of rocks and boulders NW of Badintagart
NC 328 182	Càrn nan Conbhairean	G		Cairn of the kennel boys (dog handlers)	A hill on the watershed

Grid Ref	Gaelic Name	O	Common Name	Interpretation/ Literal Translation	Comment
NC 407 177	Carraichan Dubh	G		Black peaty uneven surface	A rocky hill and the Parish Boundary
NC 411 113			Ruined castle Brough?	Ancient Dùn	On W bank of R.Cassley 8 miles from Rosehall
NC 390 007	Cathair Thurnaig			Chair of Tournaig	A round heathery knoll NNW of Wester Tournaig
NC 327 126	Cathraichean Bàna	G		White chairs (seats)	A few small knolls on the E side of Glen Oykel near Loch Ailsh
NC 437 016	Cladh a Cnòcain	G		Burying place of the little hillock	A small burial place on Cnòc nam Braithrean
NC 390 036	Clais Mhòr	G		Large hollow	A big hollow ¼ ml. In breadth about ½ mile SE of Loch na Claise Mòire
NC	Cluas na Biathainne	G		Ear of the earth worm	A small hill N of Càrn Mòr

Grid Ref	Gaelic Name	O	Common Name	Interpretation/ Literal Translation	Comment
NC 363 018	Cnòc a'Bhaid Daraich	G		Knoll of the oak wood	A little hill of oak trees
NC 350 147	Cnoc an Tosgaire	G		Knoll of the messenger	A little NW of Caplich
NC 326 145	Cnòc Fionn	G		Fair hillock (with white stones)	A heathy hillock 1084ft.
NC	Cnòc Glas an Dubh Coille	G		Grey hillock of the dark wood	A hill between Allt Dail Faid and Allt an Dubh Choille
NC	Cnoc Leacach	G		Flagstone hillock	A small hill with slabs of rock visible
NC 369 028	Cnoc Loch a'Brochain	G		Hillock of the loch of the gruel	
NC 419 084	Cnoc Mòr	G		Big hill	
NC	Cnoc nan Gamhna	G		Hillock of the stirks	A little hill S.of Coire Bog

Grid Ref	Gaelic Name	O	Common Name	Interpretation/ Literal Translation	Comment
NC 441 077	Coille Innis na Circe	G		Wood of the meadow of the moor hen. Possibly grouse	Forest surrounding Glencassley Castle
NC 403 122	Coille na Cròic	G		Wood of the antler	
NC 455 016	Coille Sròn na Croiche	G		Wood of the snout of the gallows	No known story
NC 378 112	Coira'Mheanbh	G		Hollow of the small creature	Suggest the home of the midges
NC	Coir'an Dubh Locha	G		Hollow of the black loch	A deep hollow W of Beinn Sgriobhinn E of Glencassley
NC 407 050	Coir'an Laogh	G		Hollow of the calf	A hollow surrounded by hills
NC	Coir' an Rasail	G N		Corrie of the horse field	Coire – a deep hollow often surrounded by hills. Horss vollr-horse field

Grid Ref	Gaelic Name	O	Common Name	Interpretation/ Literal Translation	Comment
NC	Cnocan nam Braithrean	G		Hill of the brothers	Hillock E of Tutim a battle was fought here between the Macleods of Assynt and Lewis and the Mackays of Strathnaver
NC 363 018	Coill'a' Bhaid Daraich	G		The oak wood	
NC 445 015	Coill a'Chnocain	G		The wood on the hillock	A birch forest
Nc 386 012	Coill'an Eas	G		Wood of the waterfall	N of Oykel Bridge
Nc 343 050	Coill'an Tosgair	G		Wood of the messenger	A birch forest
NC 394 141	Coille Dail nan Cliabh	G		Wood of the field of the creels	

Grid Ref	Gaelic Name	O	Common Name	Interpretation/ Literal Translation	Comment
NC	Coir'an Ruathair	G		Hollow of the skirmish	
NC 477 053	Coire Bog	G		Soft hollow	
NC 370 064	Coire Buidhe	G		Yellow hollow	
NC 375 080	Coire Dubh	G		Black hollow	
NC 355 086	Coire Glas	G		Grey hollow	
NC	Coire na Ceàrdaich	G		Hollow of the smithy	
NC 335 173	Coire nan Conbhairean	G		Hollow of the dog-handlers	Specifically hunting dogs
NC 314 178	Creag Bad a'Chreamh	G		Rock of the thicket of garlic	

Grid Ref	Gaelic Name	O	Common Name	Interpretation/ Literal Translation	Comment
NC	Creagan Daraich	G		Oaken rock	Rocks with stunted trees growing in the clefts
NC	Cròic Uachdarach	G		Upper antler	The highest pasture at that point
NC 424 101	Croich	G	Croick	A small settlement	A shepherd's house
NC	Dail Langwell	N		lang-vollr - long field of the dale	Pasture between Allt Langwell and R.Cassley
NC	Dail Tigh a'Chumhainn	G		Dale of the house of the narrow	Flat pasture between road and R.Oykel SE of Tigh a' Chumhain
NC 397 146	An Dail Teamhair	G	Dailteamhair	Pleasant field or dale	A house with ground attached on E side of R.Cassley SE of Duchally
NC 388 163	Dail nan Cliabh	G	Dalnaclave	The dale of the creels	Land with riverside dwelling with ground attached. Creels capturing fish in the river.

Grid Ref	Gaelic Name	O	Common Name	Interpretation/ Literal Translation	Comment
NC 449 059	Drochaid Allt an Rosail	G N		Bridge of horse field	A bridge on the Allt an Rasail
NC 409 013	Drochaid Bad air Donnadh	G		Bridge of the browned grove	A bridge on the road A837 crossing Allt Bad air Donnadh
NC 384 176	Dubh Choille	G		Black wood	A dense wood of natural growth
NC 325 165	Dubh Loch Beag	G		Little black loch	Cloud cover causes the illusion that the water surface is black
NC 431 150	Dubh Loch Mòr	G		Big black loch	See above
NC 388 170	Duchally	G	Duchally	Black wood?	From dùth- due proportion
NC 336 164	Creag an Fhir- eòin	G	Eagle rock		A rocky feature on the summit of Meall an Aonach 2345ft.

Grid Ref	Gaelic Name	O	Common Name	Interpretation/ Literal Translation	Comment
NC 396 136	Easan na Gaibhre	G		Waterfall of the goat	Two waterfalls where the R Cassley joinsb Allt na Gaibhre
NC 405 003		G?	Easter Turnaig		A riverside croft
NC 443 013	Eilean an Eòrna	G		Island of the barley	A large flat area where barley was grown
NC 450 012	Eilean an òba	G		Island of the creek	A large field partly surrounded by the old channel of R.Oykel
NC 405 300	Eilean Thurnaig		Isle of Turnaig		A sizeable island mainly pasture land in the river Oykel, between Easter&Wester Tournaig.The old channel between the island and the northern shore is dry except during floods

Grid Ref	Gaelic Name	O	Common Name	Interpretation/ Literal Translation	Comment
NC 372 042	Foinn Bheinn Mhòr	G		Large white mountain	White stone or scree as well as heath pasture
NC 303 189	Fuaran ruadh	G	Red well	A spring at the source of the river Oykel	So called because of the colour of the soil from which it springs or because of iron content in the water.
NC	Garbh Àth na Caonnaig	G		Rough ford of the fight	About ½ mile from Loch Ailsh. A rough shallow water
NC 420 012	Garbh Leathad	G		Rough hillside	The rough face of a hill
NC 370 133	Glas Choille	G		Grey wood	In this case birch wood
NC 380 135	Gleann na Muic	G		Glen of the pig	
NC 450 050	Gleann a' Charsla	G	Glen Cassley		In Gàidhlig it is glen of the castles or fortifications

Grid Ref	Gaelic Name	O	Common Name	Interpretation/ Literal Translation	Comment
NC 340 050	Gleann Oiceall	G P	Glen Oykel	Uchel , Pictish word meaning high	Watson gives Oykell as representing height
NC 396 128	Gleann Muice	G	Glenmuick	Pig glen	
NC 465 043	Gleann Rosail	G N	Glenrossal		Horse fields in the glen
NC	Innis Beith	G	Inchbay	Birchen meadow	Heathland on N.side of R.Oykel
NC 492 006	Inbhir nan Ault	G	Invernauld	At the mouth of the river	Confluence of the burns
NC 570 985	Inbhirean	G	Inveran	Little confluence	A837 crossing R shin Sinn ancient name of the river
NC 323 120	Ceann Loch Aillse	G	Kinlochailsh	At the head of the loch	A dwelling on site at the N.end of Loch Ailsh -
NC 410 127	Langwelldale	N	Langwell	Long dale	

Grid Ref	Gaelic Name	O	Common Name	Interpretation/ Literal Translation	Comment
NC	Leacan Dubh Bad an t-sagairt	G		Black Hillside of the priest's grove	In Gaidhlic Leacann means on the side of a hill, giving shelving ground
NC 395 116	Leathad a'Mheanbh Bhith	G		Hillside of the small creature	A midge area?
NC 554 985	Lèan	G N	Linsidecroy	Flax settlement from N lìn-setr. Croy is derived from Gaelic cruaidh,hard i.e. a dry site	Lèan in Gaidhlig means a swampy place the remainder of the word is Norse meaning flax land
NC 545 991	Lèan	G	Linsidemore		As above - now a crofting district
NC 371 031	Loch a'Bhrochain	G		Loch of the gruel	
NC 315 110	Loch Ailsh	G			

Grid Ref	Gaelic Name	O	Common Name	Interpretation/ Literal Translation	Comment
NC 475 087	Loch an Rasail	N		Loch of the horse field	
NC 312 232	Loch Bealach a' Mhadaidh	G		Pass of the wolf	
NC 382 063	Loch Beinn an Eòin Bheag	G		Loch of the mountain of the little birds	Ornithology territory
NC 343 175	Loch Càrn nan Conbhairean	G		Loch of the cairn of the kennel – men	
NC 353 122	Loch Meall a'Bhùiridh	G		Loch of the hill of the rutting or roaring	For example 'Poll Bùiridh ' rutting place of the deer. Loud roaring. Hunting country
NC 385 050	Loch na Claise Mòire	G		Loch of the large hollow	More correctly trenches. It is difficult to provide an accurate English equivalent.
NC 397 074	Loch na Faichde	G		Loch of the dew, hollow	

Grid Ref	Gaelic Name	O	Common Name	Interpretation/ Literal Translation	Comment
NC 334 148	Loch Sàil an Ruathair	G		Loch of the heel of the sudden onset	Ruathair a noun, a violent attack-a skirmish
NC 398 003	Loch Thurnaig				
NC 451 022	Lochan Imheir	G		Edward's little loch perhaps from a literature pen-name	Imir? – a ridge of land
NC 463 042	Lùb Bad na h-Ula	G		Bend of the tuft of rank grass. It could be from ulaidh for hidden treasure	Suggested windy spot
NC 345 128	Meall a'Bhùiridh	G		Hill of the rutting place	
NC 336 164	Meall an Aonach	G		Hill of the desert place	Steep heathy terrain
NC	Meall Donn	G		Brown hill	

Grid Ref	Gaelic Name	O	Common Name	Interpretation/ Literal Translation	Comment
NC 373 158	Mòinteach Dail nan Cliabh	G		Moss of the field of the creel	Moss meaning peat moss or moorland
NC 385 008	Oykel Bridge	P			
NC 578 950	Port na Leac	G	Invershin	Ferry at the flagstone	A shelving rock near the old inn on the Kyle of Sutherland
NC4 480 60	Rasail	N	Rossal	Norse	Horse field
NC 334 071	Salachy	G		Place of willows	A shepherd's house in Glen Oykel
NC 455 019	Sròn na Croiche	G		Snout of the gallows	A big hill
NC 345 155	Sròn Sgàile	G		Shadowed snout	Projecting part of Meall an Aonach

Grid Ref	Gaelic Name	O	Common Name	Interpretation/ Literal Translation	Comment
NC 455 011	An t-Strath Oiceall	G P	Strath Oykel		
NC 450 014	Taigh a'Chumhain	G	Tycuman	House of the narrow straight	A house on the Bonar Bridge to Ledmore road SW of Invercassley
NC	Tobar a' Chnocain	G		Well of the hillock	
NC 436 015	Tuiteam Tarbhach	G		Heavy fall	It acquired its name as a result of a battle fought here between the clans Macleod and Mackay
NC 437 104	Tuiteam	G	Tutim	Fall	
NC 396 002	Wester Turnaig				A house and croft

Modern Day Settlements

Bonar Bridge is now the largest inhabited settlement in the parish. In earlier times, before the first bridge was built, the main population was centred in the crofting districts of Airdens, Migdale and Tulloch, with the focus on the church in Migdale.

The Free Church set up a school there, as well as a Gaelic school in Airdens, before an Act of Parliament was passed making education compulsory. Now there are three churches in the district as well as the Primary School.

Migdale-Loch Migdale (NH 624 916} Henge: Cairn: Hut Circle.
An archaeological evaluation was undertaken in April 2003 as part of a Time Team programme for Channel 4 when Marion Fraser, of the history group, led the team to Càrn na Fitheach (now known as Tulloch Hill) where the well documented "Migdale Hoard" was found at the beginning of the 20th century

Rosehall – Gaelic name Innis na Lèan, a settlement situated at the head of the Kyle of Sutherland. See panels in the log cabin at the entrance to the Rosehall Forest Trail depicting archaeological evidence of habitation from earliest times. The Barracks, terraced housing, believed to be 19th century and used by tradesmen/craftsmen when roads, as we know them, were first constructed by the government.

Invershin - at the confluence of River Shin and River Oykel (River Cassley joined the Oykel at Rosehall). Today, it is a residential and farming community, including Inbhirean, Port na Leac, and Baile nan Creagan formerly, a busy township supporting a staging inn, school, railway station and in earlier times a salmon canning factory.

Inveran Bridge spanning River Shin
Inveran (Inbhirean - little confluence - River Shin with Alt na ciste dhuibhe)

Spinningdale – a crofting community, situated on the Dornoch Firth. When George Dempster was the owner of Skibo estate, in the middle of the 19th century, he built a mill in this crofting township, introducing spinning and weaving of cotton to the Highlands.
In 1953 the Scottish Hydro-Electric Company introduced electricity to Spinningdale.

The End Piece

As we acknowledged at the outset with regard to publishing a book of place names of our parish, we have employed various disciplines.

In archaeological terms the available documentation indicates that the area had many fortifications such as Gleann a'Charsla (Glen Cassley) which literal translation is, glen of castles and fortifications, and words such as ràth and dùn.

We worked from a Gaelic perspective although Old Norse derivations are applied in some instances as a result of early Viking invasions.

The movement of peoples over the centuries embraces many languages including Pictish, Welsh, Scots, English and French affecting etymology, and as well as the linguistic discipline employed we found that geography overlaps history when maps were used for recording accurate locations.

In this regard we are grateful to Ordnance Survey.

Geography apart, an accurate interpretation requires a great deal of research, this we discovered when considering Abhainn Sin (River Shin) which is of Pre-Celtic origin, and hydronomy came into play taking up several pages of the book when it was found that many place names are linguistically linked to water of one category or another.

The Scots word, burn, means a stream in English. If as in English using a descriptive compound word the qualifying element precedes the word, "burn" in this case, very often taking the name from the terrain the water passes through, for example, Migdale Burn.

There are some duplications of words used to explain fully and beyond doubt, the exact meaning in the landscape context, but where there is more than one place with the same original name description, we have not recorded each place.

There are many big hills named Càrn Mòr so, for the record, here is a picture of Càrn Mòr situated in the largest inhabited settlement in the Parish of Creich. Much of the arable land belonging to this holding has been taken over to provide Local Authority Housing in the village called Bonar Bridge. Since Càrn Mòr is situated in the district of Tulloch the first street placed on the march of that land was named Tulloch Road.

Bonar Bridge - Site of early19th century ford - An àth

Bonar Bridge - Where the Kyle of Sutherland becomes the Dornoch Firth

Acharry - Route taken by Danish invaders to battle at Tulloch

Seana Bhaile & Druim Bàn

Migdale Brae - Where Airdens & Migdale Meet

Path to Achinduich by Loch Larro with snow-clad Ben More

Deserted township at Loch Laro

Corn-drying kiln

Allt na Ciste Dubh

Badbea - Several crofts here above Loch Migdale

Balblair - a small estate

Loch End & Culnara

Standing stone commemorating Norse commander

Flat farmland known as Fload

Garvary - last house before Rogart boundary

Loch Buidhe - note yellow reflection

Loch Laggan & Meall Diolaid (The Saddle)

Rivaig - Creich/Dornoch parish boundary

Site of battle culminating at Drumliath

ALTAS crofting communities

Wildlife in Glenrossal

Glen Cassley castle

River Cassley joins the The Oykel at Rosehall

Glen Cassley

Original Bridge at Oykel

Footbridge & ford over River Oykel at Tutim

The Free Church, Migdale with its adjoining school buildings

Looking out to the Parish of Assynt